COOKING
with the
BAD GUYS

COOKING
with the
BAD GUYS

Recipes from the World's Most
Notorious Kitchens

DON ABEL

THE OVERLOOK PRESS

WOODSTOCK • NEW YORK

First published in 1995 by
The Overlook Press
Lewis Hollow Road
Woodstock, New York 12498

PHOTO CREDITS: Victoriano Huerta courtesy UPI/Bettmann; Tomàs de
Torquemada and Blackbeard courtesy The Bettmann Archive; Al Capone,
Rasputin, Jack the Ripper, Attila the Hun and Salome courtesy Archive
Photos, Marie Antoinette courtesy Stock Montage, Inc.; General Custer
courtesy the Library of Congress

Library of Congress Cataloging-in-Publication Data

Abel, Don
Cooking with the bad guys : recipes from the world's most
notorious kitchens / Don Abel. 1. Cookery. 2. Cookery–Humor. I. Title.
TX714.A36 1994   641.5'0207–dc20   94-18364
ISBN 0-87951-564-3
1 3 5 7 9 8 6 4 2

BOOK DESIGN BY BERNARD SCHLEIFER
Printed in the United States of America

Dedication

For my loving, sexy, and supportive wife Frankie, mother of our sons Ross Zachary and Don Arthur. All good eaters, and not a "bad guy" in the bunch.

Contents

"Grub first, then ethics."
—BERTOLT BRECHT

"A man who can dominate a London dinner table can dominate the world."
—OSCAR WILDE

"I believe I once considerably scandalized her by declaring that clear soup was a more important factor in life than a clear conscience."
—SAKI

Thundering herds.

Backroom manipulations.

Wholesale destruction.

Bald-faced lies.

Bad guys (and gals) have created vast empires, brought enemies to ruin, demolished cities, stolen state secrets, and generally wreaked havoc over the centuries. But, they had to eat sometime . . .

Salome

"Before I was born my mother was in great agony of spirit and in a tragic situation. She could take no food except iced oysters and champagne. If people ask me when I began to dance, I reply, "In my mother's womb, probably as a result of the oysters and champagne—the food of Aphrodite."
—Isadora Duncan

SALOME (first century A.D.) was the daughter of Herodias and the step-daughter of Herod Antipas, governor of Galilee and Perea. On good authority (Matthew 14:6–12 and Mark 6:22–8) Salome was the original femme fatale (emphasis on the fatale) and is credited with the beheading of John the Baptist, one of her more charming accomplishments.

The story goes that she danced at a birthday party for her stepfather, Herod. A provocative dance by any standards and particularly by those of the first century, her choreography–a strategic use of seven veils–pleased Herod so much he offered Salome anything she wanted. At her mother's suggestion–Herodias had an old ax to grind with John, who had spoken out against her incestuous marriage to Herod (she had previously been married to Herod's brother Philip, which ran counter to the law of the day)–she requested the head of John the Baptist. Herod ordered John beheaded and sent Salome his head on a platter.

Matthew's account of the story has Herod sorry about the whole thing, but, well, a promise is a promise. In Mark's version, Herod even offered Salome "half my kingdom" instead. She declined.

Salome was a woman of strong and decadent appetites, and appropriately, the recipes here are representative of a particularly wealthy and experienced palate during Old Testament times.

T   H   E   •   R   E   C   I   P   E   S

Seven-Veil Salad
Pickled Vegetables
Savory Lamb Casserole
Galilee Bread
Fatale-*ly Delicious Almond Dessert*

SEVEN-VEIL SALAD

1 head lettuce (romaine)
2 cucumbers, peeled and sliced
½ cup green onions, chopped
¼ cup parsley, minced
¼ cup dill, chopped
¾ cup sesame oil or
   olive oil

⅓ cup lemon juice
1 teaspoon salt
¼ teaspoon black pepper
2 cloves garlic, minced
¼ pound feta cheese

Wash and dry the lettuce, then tear into bite-sized pieces. Combine in a bowl with peeled and sliced vegetables and herbs.

Beat together oil, lemon juice, salt, pepper, and minced garlic. Before serving, mix the dressing with the vegetables, and add crumbled feta cheese to top. SERVES 6

PICKLED VEGETABLES

4 turnips	4 cups water
3 cups cabbage, shredded	5 cloves garlic, minced
1½ cups celery, sliced	3 cups white vinegar
¾ cup salt	3 tablespoons pickling spice

Skin the turnips, then cut in half lengthwise. Slice thinly. Mix with shredded cabbage and sliced celery.

In a large glass jar, dissolve salt in water. Add the vegetables and minced garlic. Mix the vinegar and pickling spice with the salt solution. Cover the jar tightly with the lid and let stand 3 to 4 days. Chill before serving. SERVES 6 (2 PINTS)

SAVORY LAMB CASSEROLE

FILLING

2 tablespoons sesame oil	½ teaspoon salt
¾ cup onions, chopped	¼ teaspoon black pepper
½ pound ground lamb	¼ cup pine nuts

Heat oil in skillet, brown chopped onions. Add lamb, salt and pepper. Cook, stirring frequently, for 5 minutes. Add the pine nuts. Cook, stirring frequently, until browned.

WHEAT MIXTURE

1 pound finely ground wheat flour	½ teaspoon black pepper
2 pounds twice-ground lamb	¼ teaspoon cinnamon
½ cup onions, grated	¼ cup ice water
2 teaspoons salt	½ cup melted butter

Barely cover wheat with cold water and soak for 30 minutes, kneading it several times. Drain, then mix in lamb, onions, salt, pepper, and cinnamon. Knead for an additional few minutes, then put through the fine blade of a food chopper, adding ¼ cup ice water while grinding.

Pat half the wheat mixture into a greased 9-inch by 12-inch baking pan. Spread the filling over it. Cover with the remaining wheat mixture, pressing down until firm. With a sharp knife, cut diagonal lines across the top to form a diamond pattern. Pour the melted butter over the top, and bake at 400° for 30 minutes. Reduce heat to 350°, and bake an additional 30 minutes. Cut into squares and serve hot. SERVES 6

GALILEE BREAD

1¼ cups lukewarm water	1 teaspoon salt
1 package active-dry yeast	2 tablespoons olive oil
4 cups flour	½ cup flour for baking

Pour ¼ cup of water into a bowl; add the yeast. Let stand 5 minutes, then stir until dissolved.

Put the 4 cups of flour and the salt into a large bowl and make a well in the center. Pour the oil, the remaining water, and the yeast mixture into the well. Mix the ingredients in the well, then work in the flour with fingers until a dough is formed. (If too stiff, add a little more warm water.) Turn out the dough onto a lightly floured surface, and knead until smooth and elastic, about 15 minutes. Shape the dough into a ball and place it in a lightly oiled bowl. Cover with a towel and keep in a warm place until doubled in bulk, about 1 hour.

Punch the dough down sharply with your hand and divide into 4 pieces, shaping each piece into a ball. Cover with a towel and let stand 30 minutes.

Use three 14-inch by 17-inch baking sheets and sprinkle each with ⅓ of the flour. (If you have one oven, you'll have to bake one pan at a time.) Roll each ball of dough into a thin circle, about 7 inches in diameter. Put two pieces on each baking sheet. Cover with a towel, and let stand for 30 minutes.

Preheat the oven to 500°. Bake the bread on the lowest level of the oven for 5 minutes, then raise to the next level and bake 5 minutes more, or until golden brown. Remove the breads from the pan and wrap in foil. The breads will be flat, but higher on the rim, and flat in the middle. Serve warm.

FATALE-LY DELICIOUS ALMOND DESSERT

1 cup sugar
1 cup honey
2 cups water
½ teaspoon cinnamon

¼ pound butter
½ cup almonds, finely ground
1 cup raw cream of wheat

Combine the sugar, honey, water, and cinnamon in a saucepan. Bring to a boil and cook over low heat for 20 minutes. While the syrup is cooking, melt the butter in a skillet and add the almonds and cream of wheat. Cook over low heat, stirring constantly until browned.

Add the skillet contents to the syrup after the syrup has cooked 20 minutes. Mix well, cover, and cook for 15 minutes, stirring occasionally. Pour into a buttered 8-inch by 10-inch shallow pan. Cool. Cut into squares and sprinkle with cinnamon. SERVES 6

Attíla the Hun

"Give them great meals of beef and iron and steel, and they will act like wolves and fight like devils."
—WILLIAM SHAKESPEARE

ATTILA THE HUN® (c. 406–453). More than any other bad guy, his name says villainy. He is the Kleenex® of criminals, the Xerox® of xenophobic maurauders. But what did he do to earn such a rep?

Attila was king of the Huns, a nomadic race with its origins in central Asia. Because of Attila's activities as a conqueror of note, he became known as the "Scourge of God." By all reports, he had a keen, predatory mind and a dominating personality; as far as barbarians go, Attila was arguably the top barbarian of all time.

In 434, Attila and his brother Bleda negotiated a treaty with the Eastern Roman emperor Theodosius II and received an annual tribute of about 700 pounds of gold (if gold was selling on the world market at $350 a troy ounce, 700 pounds would come to about $2,940,000 – not bad for a barbarian).

After six years of peace (about $17,640,000 of tribute), Attila invaded Theodosius II's empire anyway, destroying numerous major cities and defeating several imperial armies. After another treaty (and payment of more tribute) peace was made – or bought – again.

In 445, Attila murdered his brother Bleda and launched a new campaign against the Roman Empire. He forced the emperor to concede large areas of land south of the Danube to the Huns and extorted a promise of an additional tribute. This systematic blackmail came to an end with the death of Theodosius II. Marcian, his successor, refused to pay the Huns any money, and Attila, now bored with the devastated eastern provinces, which were hardly worth further plundering, turned his attention westward.

The nomad's gastronomic fare was usually limited to what could be eaten while on horseback. Attila's ambition brought him far enough west to be influenced by the civilized and sophisticated palates of the Germans and the Romans, and his own palate got correspondingly pickier. For instance, he began demanding *cooked* meat . . .

T H E • R E C I P E S

Bacon Leek Soup
Rabbit in Yogurt
Conqueror's Cabbage with Dill and Sour Cream
"Scourge of God" White Beans
Noodle Pudding

BACON LEEK SOUP

6 *medium leeks, chopped*
6¼ *cups beef stock (or bouillon)*
¾ *teaspoon salt*
½ *teaspoon black pepper*
8 *ounces bacon*

6 *onions*
9 *ounces smoked ham*
½ *cup fresh parsley*
½ *cup fresh chives*
¼ *cup chervil*

Wash the leeks well. Using the white parts only of the leeks, cut into cubes. Wash and chop the parsley. Place the vegetables in a saucepan and add stock. Bring to a boil over high heat, then reduce heat and simmer, partially covered, for 15 minutes or until the leeks are cooked.

Remove the pan from the heat, and press the liquid and vegetables through a sieve. Season with the salt and pepper, and keep hot.

Cut the bacon into small cubes. Peel and chop the onions, and cut the smoked ham into small strips. Lightly sauté the bacon in a large skillet for 15 minutes. Add the onions, and sauté for a few more minutes. Add the smoked ham and continue cooking, stirring frequently, until the mixture becomes lightly browned.

Spoon the sautéed ingredients on top of the hot soup, garnish with chopped fresh chives and chervil, and serve immediately. SERVES 6

RABBIT IN YOGURT

saddle and hind legs of
   2 rabbits
8 slices bacon
½ teaspoon salt
½ teaspoon pepper
2 onions
2 carrots
½ cup butter

1 bay leaf
3 sprigs parsley
1 sprig thyme
¾ cup red wine
¾ cup yogurt
¾ cup dairy sour cream
½ cup water

Preheat oven to 375°. Remove all tendons and skin from the rabbit (they tend to harden during cooking). Rinse and dry the pieces thoroughly. Cut the bacon into thin strips. Make small slits with the point of a knife in rabbit, and insert the bacon strips. Sprinkle the pieces with salt and pepper.

Peel and slice the onions and carrots. Melt the butter in a roasting pan, and add the rabbit, onion, carrot, 1 bay leaf, 3 sprigs of parsley, 1 sprig of thyme, and wine. Add the yogurt and sour cream.

Place pan in the center of a preheated oven (375°), and roast for 1½ to 2 hours, basting frequently. Lift the rabbit from the pan and cut into slices. Keep hot in a covered dish while preparing the sauce.

To make the sauce, add ½ cup water to the liquid remaining in the roasting pan, and bring to a boil. Stir until well blended. Strain the sauce over the rabbit, and serve hot. SERVES 6

CONQUEROR'S CABBAGE
WITH DILL AND SOUR CREAM

3 *pounds cabbage*
   salt
¼ *teaspoon caraway seeds*
2 *tablespoons butter*

1 *small onion*
2 *tablespoons flour*
2 *tablespoons fresh dill*
2 *tablespoons sour cream*

Clean and core the cabbage, and slice it into ¼ inch thick pieces. Cook in rapidly boiling salted water with caraway seeds until tender but still firm, about 10 minutes. Drain, reserving 2 cups of the cooking liquid for the sauce. Melt the butter in a heavy saucepan over low heat, and sauté the onion until the pieces wilt.

Stir the flour into the sautéed onions, and cook for 2 to 3 minutes. Gradually add ½ cup of the cabbage broth, then stir in up to 1½ cups more broth to make a thin sauce. Let sauce simmer, stirring occasionally, for 10 minutes. (If the sauce seems floury, simmer a little longer.) When the sauce is done, remove from heat, add the drained cabbage and dill, and let it cool. When the sauce is barely lukewarm, pour a little into the sour cream, then pour the mixed sour cream back into the cabbage. Reheat to simmering and serve. SERVES 6.

"SCOURGE OF GOD" WHITE BEANS

1 pound northern or navy beans	2 tablespoons butter
1½ teaspoons salt	¼ cup onions, chopped
1 bay leaf	1½ teaspoons Hungarian paprika
1 carrot	
1 leek	2 tablespoons parsley, chopped
1 clove garlic	2 tablespoons flour
½ pound smoked bacon (or ham or pork chop)	½ cup sour cream
	1 tablespoon vinegar

Wash the beans, and soak them overnight in cold water. Drain and rinse the beans, and put in a clean pot. Add the salt, bay leaf, carrot, leek, whole garlic, and smoked meat. Pour on enough water to barely cover the beans and meat, and bring to a simmer. Cook slowly, partially covered, for 2½ to 3 hours, or until the beans are tender, adding more boiling water as necessary to keep them covered. When beans are done, discard the carrot, leek, and garlic. Put the meat in a side dish and drain off the cooking liquid to use in the sauce.

Melt the butter in a saucepan over low heat. Sauté the onions until they wilt, then add the paprika and chopped parsley and stir in 2 tablespoons flour. Cook for 2–3 minutes, then gradually stir in 2 cups of the bean cooking liquid. Pour the sauce into the beans, blend, and simmer for another 10 minutes. (If the sauce is too thick, add more of the bean cooking liquid.) Let the beans cool. Stir some of the beans into the sour cream, then slowly pour the sour cream mixture into the bean pot. Mix in the vinegar, and taste for seasoning. Cut the meat into bite-sized pieces, add it to the beans, and serve.

SERVES 6-8.

NOODLE PUDDING

3 tablespoons butter
3 tablespoons bread crumbs
½ pound egg noodles
⅓ cup sugar
3 eggs

1 teaspoon cinnamon
2 cups cottage cheese
½ cup yellow raisins
½ cup chopped nuts
½ cup apricot filling
(or jam)

Lightly grease a 1½-quart baking dish with some of the butter, then sprinkle the bottom and sides with bread crumbs, shaking out the excess.

Cook the noodles according to the package directions, then drain and toss noodles with the rest of the butter. Beat the sugar and eggs together, and add the cinnamon. Stir in the cottage cheese, then the raisins and nuts. Add the noodles, and turn them carefully so all are coated.

Preheat the oven to 350°. Pour one-half of the mixture into the baking dish, spread the layer with apricot filling, then pour the rest on top. Bake for 30 minutes or until the pudding is set and the top is golden brown. Serve hot from the casserole. SERVES 6.

Tomás de Torquemada

"After a good dinner, one can forgive anybody, even one's own relations."
—OSCAR WILDE

TOMÁS DE TORQUEMADA (1420–1498), a veritable model of fanaticism and persecution, was appointed to the position of grand inquisitor in 1487 by Ferdinand and Isabella, the king and queen of Spain. He used his power to exile 200,000 people from Spain and burn over 2,000 accused heretics.

Although said to be of Jewish descent, Torquemada instigated attacks on Orthodox Jews and Jews who had converted to Christianity. He pushed vigorously for the prosecution of Moors, apostate Christians, witches, crypto-Jews and other "spiritual offenders," a category that could include just about anybody he wasn't fond of.

The Inquisition officially began in Europe around 1232 with Pope Gregory IX, as a strategy of the Roman Catholic Church to combat heresy. In the late fifteenth century Ferdinand and Isabella acquired from Pope Sixtus IV the right to appoint all the higher ecclesiastical officers in Spain, thereby guaranteeing their loyalty to the crown. With Torquemada at the helm, the Inquisition was often used for political manipulation; as a result, the Church and Crown, powerful and persuasive bed partners, could effectively and efficiently dispose of any and all opposition.

Food was often used as evidence of apostasy: kosher butchering, eating meat during Lent, or keeping the fast of Rebeaso was enough to bring a "heretic" up before the Inquisition.

La Mancha Soup
Bewitching Chicken with Orange and Mint
Potatoes with Garlic Mayonnaise
Sponge Cake with Almonds

LA MANCHA SOUP

4 cloves garlic
6 slices bread
8 ounces thick-sliced bacon
4 ounces smoked ham
4 ounces ground pork

6 tablespoons olive oil
½ cup all-purpose flour
1 teaspoon paprika
½ teaspoon pepper
2 teaspoons salt
8 cups water

Peel and halve the garlic cloves. Cut the bread, bacon, and ham into ½-inch cubes. Heat the oil in a saucepan and sauté the garlic cloves until they begin to brown. Add the bacon, ham, and pork; sauté for about 5 minutes. Remove with a perforated spoon and drain on paper towels. Add the cubed bread and sauté until crisp and golden brown. Remove with a perforated spoon and drain on paper towels.

Add the flour, paprika, pepper, and salt to the oil remaining in the pan. Cook for 5 minutes, stirring constantly. Add the water gradually, stirring well after each addition. Bring to a boil and cook for 15 minutes, stirring constantly. Add the bread cubes, garlic, bacon, ham, and pork. Boil for an additional 5 minutes, then serve in deep soup bowls. SERVES 6

BEWITCHING CHICKEN WITH
ORANGE AND MINT

9 ounces boneless chicken breasts,
   skinned
salt
freshly ground black pepper
3 tablespoons butter

1 cup freshly squeezed orange juice
2 tablespoons chopped fresh mint
   sprigs of mint and orange slices,
    to garnish

Season chicken breasts with salt and pepper. Melt 2 tablespoons of butter in a pan and sauté the chicken pieces for about 4 minutes, turning once.

Add the orange juice, bring to a simmer, then cover and cook for 8 to 10 minutes. When the chicken is almost tender, add the chopped mint and 1 tablespoon of butter to thicken the sauce.

Serve with some sprigs of mint and sliced orange. SERVES 6

POTATOES WITH GARLIC MAYONNAISE

2 lbs. new potatoes, scrubbed but
   not peeled
6 tablespoons olive oil
3 teaspoons wine vinegar
   salt

freshly ground black pepper
8 tablespoons garlic mayonnaise
   (see below)
1 teaspoon paprika

Cook potatoes in lightly salted boiling water until tender. Drain, then cut into bite-sized pieces.

Mix together the oil and vinegar with some salt and pepper. Add the garlic mayonnaise and mix in the paprika, reserving a pinch or two for garnishing, while the potatoes are still warm. Chill before serving, then top with the reserved paprika.
SERVES 6

GARLIC MAYONNAISE (ALIOLI)

4 cloves of garlic, peeled
2 egg yolks
   pinch of salt

pinch of white pepper
1 cup olive oil

Crush the garlic until completely pulverized using a large pestle and mortar, then place into a large bowl. Add the egg yolks, salt, and pepper and stir to combine. Using a hand whisk, stir the egg mixture continuously while adding the olive oil, drop by drop to begin with, then gradually building up to a slow drizzle, until mixture is thick. Adjust the seasoning to taste.

You can also make this in a food processor or blender. Start by mixing together the garlic, egg yolks, and seasoning, adding the oil in a slow drizzle while the machine is running.

SPONGE CAKE
WITH ALMONDS

1¼ cups sugar	⅔ cup cornstarch
6 eggs	2 tablespoons butter, melted
dash of salt	½ cup flaked almonds
1 cup all-purpose flour	3 tablespoons sugar

Preheat oven to 350°. Place the sugar, eggs, and salt in a bowl, preferably copper, over a saucepan of simmering water. Beat lightly until the mixture begins to thicken, then remove from heat and continue to beat until mixture is very thick and almost white in color. Sift the flour with the cornstarch, then sift again into the egg mixture, and fold in gently, using a metal spoon. Fold in the melted butter.

Pour the mixture into 2 lined, buttered, and floured 9-inch round layer cake pans; smooth with a spatula, then top with almonds and 3 tablespoons sugar, evenly distributed. Bake in a preheated oven (350°) for 35 to 40 minutes. Let stand in the pans to cool for 5 minutes, then turn onto a rack, and set aside to cool completely. MAKES 2 9-INCH CAKES

Blackbeard
the Pírate

EDWARD TEACH (d. 1718), better known as Blackbeard, turned to piracy as a full-time profession after a longtime career as a privateer during the War of the Spanish Succession (1701–1713). He and his band preyed on the trade ships between the Caribbean and the Atlantic Coast of North America.

Blackbeard was a big man, standing six feet four inches and weighing in at 250 pounds, with a deep bass voice that reverberated loudly. He received his nickname from his great black beard that grew thick to his waist – no surprise here. On special occasions he tied colorful ribbons in his beard.

Dressed in a long overcoat and breeches, Blackbeard stuck slow burning matches in the crown of his wide-brimmed hat and attached more to his beard. This massive man, flames and smoke billowing from his hat and beard, cutlass in one hand, pistol in the other – with additional pistols stashed in his belt and pockets – would climb over the side of his victims' ships, shouting obscenities and looking oddly festive and intimidating at the same time.

Blackbeard is also legendary for his original, and rather final, method of divesting himself of wives. It was said that as he grew tired of each young wife, he would lure her into his treasure room and, as she exclaimed over the chests heaped with gold and jewels, would laugh in his booming voice and slip out the door, locking it behind him. He married a total of fourteen times using this effective technique.

On November 22, 1718, Edward Teach met his end via Lieutenant Robert Maynard of His Majesty's Navy. Edward, having drunk perhaps a little too much rum prior to the confrontation, was felled with twenty-five wounds. The lieutenant, to prove he had killed Blackbeard, decapitated the pirate and spiked his head to his bowsprit, resulting in a maruader's idea of the ultimate hood ornament.

Blackbeard was a hearty eater with relatively simple tastes. The Caribbean food he ate went well with his beverage of choice, rum: hot or cold, straight or mixed, light or dark. Just a lot of it.

T H E • R E C I P E S

Flamed Pork Appetizer
Swashbuckling Conch Chowder
Lime-Broiled Grouper
Akkras
Baked Mashed Potatoes with Pineapple
Papaya-Coconut Pie

FLAMED PORK APPETIZER

1-pound pork roast, cooked
1 *onion*
1 *green pepper*
1 *tablespoon Worcestershire sauce*

½ *cup rum*
½ *teaspoon ground ginger*
bread and crackers

Chop meat coarsely with onion and green pepper. Add the Worcestershire sauce. Warm a large metal cooking spoon or ladle, pour the rum into the spoon, and light the rum. Then pour the burning rum over the chopped meat, shaking the mixture until the rum has burned all of it. Let the rum burn out completely. Add the ginger and serve on bread or crackers. SERVES 6

Note: The "buccaneer" means someone who "boucans" or barbecues meat, which is how the West Indian buccaneers cooked the wild hogs, island turkey, ducks, and chickens they killed. Fresh meat had to be cooked quickly before it spoiled in the hot Caribbean sun.

SWASHBUCKLING CONCH CHOWDER

1 *pound fresh conch*	½ *cup carrots, diced*
juice of 3 fresh limes	½ *cup celery, chopped*
6 *slices bacon*	1 *tablespoon Worcestershire sauce*
¼ *cup onion, chopped*	1 *teaspoon salt*
2 *cups water*	½ *teaspoon pepper*
4 *tomatoes, diced*	½ *teaspoon thyme*
1 *cup potatoes, diced*	1 *cup cooked pigeon peas*

Tenderize fresh conch by placing fillets between two pieces of waxed paper, then cover with cheesecloth. With wooden tenderizer (or small hammer) thoroughly pound the conch for at least 10 minutes. Cut tenderized conch into 1-inch pieces and let soak in small bowl with lime juice. Set aside.

Fry bacon until crisp, then break into small pieces. In pan with bacon add chopped onion; cook until tender. Put in large pot, then add water, diced tomatoes, potatoes, carrots, chopped celery, Worcestershire sauce, and seasonings. Cover and simmer 40 minutes (or until vegetables are tender). Add precooked pigeon peas and conch, simmer for 15 additional minutes. (Conch will not flake like other fish when done.)

SERVES 6

LIME-BROILED GROUPER

2 pounds fresh grouper fillets
2 cloves garlic, finely chopped
½ cup melted butter
2 tablespoons fresh lime juice

¼ teaspoon salt
¼ teaspoon pepper
1 teaspoon paprika

Place fresh grouper fillets on oiled broiler pan. Combine finely chopped garlic with melted butter, lime juice, salt, and pepper and brush on fish. Sprinkle with paprika. Broil 4 or 5 inches from heat, basting often, until fish is tender in its thickest part (time varies with cut of fish). SERVES 6

AKKRAS

2¼ cups black-eyed peas
½ teaspoon salt
6 cups water

1 green pepper, diced
cooking oil

Soak the peas overnight in water, then drain and puree in a blender. Add enough water to help grind, then stir in salt and pepper. Heat a skillet with enough oil to cover the bottom. Drop the peas by a tablespoon into the hot oil. Brown on both sides, then drain. Serve hot. SERVES 6

BAKED MASHED POTATOES
WITH PINEAPPLE

4 cups cooked mashed potatoes
2 medium onions, chopped
1 celery stalk, chopped
½ green pepper, chopped
8 tablespoons cooking oil
½ cup tomato sauce

3 tablespoons dried parsley
½ cup raisins
⅓ cup brown sugar
2 eggs, mixed
1 cup milk
1 fresh pineapple

Prepare mashed potatoes, using your favorite recipe. Set aside. Brown the chopped onions, celery, and green pepper with 4 tablespoons of cooking oil in a preheated oven (325°). Then add the tomato sauce, dried parsley, raisins, brown sugar, and mixed eggs. Stir well. Add potatoes, remaining cooking oil, and milk. Spread in shallow baking dish and bake for 45 minutes.

Serve warm with sliced fresh pineapple. SERVES 6

PAPAYA-COCONUT PIE

2 fresh papayas, peeled, seeded,
    and cubed
1 cup shredded coconut
1 cup sugar
2 eggs, beaten

1 cup evaporated milk
½ teaspoon nutmeg
½ teaspoon cinnamon
1 8-inch unbaked pastry shell
    (see below)

Combine the cubed papayas, shredded coconut, sugar, beaten eggs, milk, nutmeg, and cinnamon. Pour into pie shell and bake in preheated oven (375°) for 10 minutes. Then reduce heat to 325° and bake an additional 35 minutes or until the filling is set. Serve chilled. SERVES 6

PASTRY SHELLS

2 cups all-purpose flour
1 teaspoon salt

⅔ cup shortening
6 teaspoons cold water

Stir flour and salt together, mix in shortening with large fork, and blend until all pieces are the size of small peas. Sprinkle 1 tablespoon of water over part of mixture. Toss with fork, push to side of bowl. Repeat until all of mixture is moist.

Divide dough into 2 balls, and flatten on lightly floured surface by pressing with edge of hand. Roll with a rolling pin from center to edge till ⅛-inch thick. Fit pastry into pie plates and trim ½ inch beyond edge, fold under, and flute edge. MAKES 2 8-INCH SHELLS (UNBAKED)

Maríe Antoínette

"At length I recollected the thoughtless saying of a great princess, who, on being informed that the country people had no bread, replied 'Let them eat cake.' "
—JEAN-JACQUES ROUSSEAU, Les Confessions

"Cake is at once America's favorite food and premier art form."
—MARCEL DUCHAMP

MARIE ANTOINETTE (1755–1793) was the queen consort of King Louis XVI of France. During her brief tenure in this role, she managed to antagonize nearly everyone at court and about twenty million French citizens to boot.

The original "shop till you drop" poster child, Marie added to the problems of Louis's heavily burdened treasury by her extravagance. Marie curtailed her shopping and social life slightly after the birth of her son, Louis Joseph, concentrating her efforts instead on meddling in affairs of state.

On August 25, 1785, a great reception was held at Versailles to celebrate the birthday of Louis XVI. All the courtiers and important people in France had been invited. A tall, broad-shouldered man burst through the crowd holding above his head a bouquet of little purple flowers. Reaching the king's side, the man—Monsieur Antoine-Auguste Parmentier—gracefully bowed and held out the flowers. "Sire," he said, "from now on famine is impossible." Parmentier had brought the blossoms of the potato, soon to become the French national vegetable.

In August 1793, Marie had an appointment with the guillotine that couldn't be cancelled. The French Revolution was over for Marie Antoinette.

Asparagus with Hollandaise
Louis's Lobster Bisque
Parmentier's Potato Quiche
Peas French-style
"Let Them Eat (Rum) Cake"

ASPARAGUS WITH HOLLANDAISE

2 **bundles asparagus (about 40 stalks in each)**

hollandaise sauce (see below)

Trim the asparagus, remove any hard stems, and clean well in cold water. Cook in boiling salted water to cover for 15 to 20 minutes or until just tender. Drain.

Serve asparagus individually on heated serving plates with a spoonful of hollandaise sauce at one end. SERVES 6

HOLLANDAISE SAUCE

juice of 1 lemon
2 *teaspoons water*
2 *egg yolks*

8 *tablespoons butter*
salt
cayenne pepper

Place the lemon juice and water in a small bowl. Put the bowl over a saucepan of simmering water (do not let it touch the water). Add the egg yolks and 1 tablespoon butter. Whisk very thoroughly until stiff.

Remove the saucepan from the heat, and add the remaining butter in very small pieces, whisking all the time. Season to taste with salt and cayenne pepper.

LOUIS'S LOBSTER BISQUE

1 large carrot, peeled and
    chopped
1 large onion, diced
4 tablespoons butter
1 small lobster
4 tablespoons brandy
1½ cups white wine

½ cup rice
7½ cups Louis XVI Bouillon
¾ cup light cream
salt
cayenne pepper
parsley for garnish

Peel and chop the carrot and onion into small pieces. Melt half of the butter in a large saucepan, add the vegetables, and cook gently, stirring, for 2 to 3 minutes. Split the lobster in half lengthwise and place it, cut side down, on the vegetables. Cover the pan and cook for 2 minutes.

Heat the brandy, ignite, and pour over the lobster with the wine.

Cover the saucepan tightly, and cook very gently for 15 minutes, lightly shaking the pan occasionally.

Cook the rice in 2½ cups boiling Louis XVI Bouillon for about 30 minutes or until very soft.

Shell the lobster, cut up the meat, and place in a bowl with drained vegetables (reserve liquid) and rice. Pound thoroughly to a soft pulp. (This can be done in an electric blender; add the reserved liquid for this process.) If done by hand, add the reserved liquid after the pounding is completed.

Add 1½ cups bouillon and sieve.

Add the remaining bouillon, pour into a clean saucepan. Reheat and whisk in the remaining butter in small pieces. Add the cream, then season with salt and cayenne pepper. Reheat, if necessary, without boiling.

Serve hot, garnished with a small sprig of parsley. SERVES 6

LOUIS XVI BOUILLON

5 cups water	2 shallots
2½ cups white wine	1 teaspoon salt
1 onion	6 white peppercorns

Slice onion thinly and chop shallots, then place all the ingredients into a saucepan. Cover, bring to a boil, and simmer for 30 to 40 minutes. Strain.

Use as required.

PARMENTIER'S POTATO QUICHE

1 pound potatoes, boiled
¼ cup butter
2 tablespoons flour
½ cup heavy cream

2 slices bacon, chopped
1 clove garlic, crushed
2 ounces Gruyère cheese, grated

Peel and dry-mash the potatoes, and mix with the butter and sifted flour. Knead until you have a firm dough. Roll it out ¼ inch thick, and lay it in a buttered and floured pie or quiche pan. Prick the base a few times with a fork, and fill with the cream and bacon, and stir in the garlic. Sprinkle the top with the cheese, and bake at 400° for about 20 minutes. Serve hot or cold. SERVES 4-6

PEAS FRENCH-STYLE

4 *tablespoons butter*
6 *small onions, sliced*
6 *lettuce leaves, finely shredded*
½ *teaspoon salt*
¼ *teaspoon black pepper*
1 *sprig parsley*

1 *sprig mint*
2 *teaspoons sugar*
1 *pound shelled peas*
¾ *cup water*
1 *teaspoon all-purpose flour*

Melt 3 tablespoons butter in a large saucepan, add the sliced onions, finely shredded lettuce, salt, pepper, parsley, mint, sugar, and peas. Stir in water, bring to a boil; cover and simmer gently for about 20 minutes or until the peas are very tender.

Remove and discard the parsley and mint. Cream the flour and 1 tablespoon butter together thoroughly, and add to the peas in small pieces. Stir gently with a wooden spoon, heating slowly until liquid is thickened.

Serve hot. SERVES 6

"LET THEM EAT (RUM) CAKE"

1 tablespoon dried yeast	*8 tablespoons butter*
½ cup milk, warmed	*⅔ cup currants*
2 cups all-purpose flour	*4 tablespoons honey*
½ teaspoon salt	*rum to taste*
2 tablespoons sugar	*3 tablespoons apricot jam*
4 eggs, beaten	*crème fraîche (see below)*

Stir the yeast into the milk. Place ½ cup of flour into a mixing bowl, add the milk and yeast, and beat well with a wooden spoon to a smooth batter. Allow to stand in a warm place until frothy. (This will be about 30 minutes.)

Put the remaining 1½ cups of flour into a bowl with the salt, sugar, beaten eggs, butter, and currants. Add the yeast mixture. Mix and beat well for 3 to 4 minutes.

Grease a 9-inch spring form pan. Fill with the yeast mixture, cover with a cloth, and allow to rise in a warm place.

Bake at the top of oven at 400° for 15 to 20 minutes. Cool for a few minutes, then turn out onto a wire rack with a tray underneath.

Place the honey in a small saucepan with 4 tablespoons water and rum to taste. Heat until blended and syrupy, stirring constantly. Pour the syrup over the warm cake, soaking it thoroughly.

Place the apricot jam in a small saucepan with 4 tablespoons water. Heat gently while stirring. Sieve. Brush the glaze generously over the cake. Cool, then transfer cake to a serving plate and top with crème fraîche. MAKES 1 9-INCH CAKE

CRÈME FRAÎCHE

1 cup heavy cream (not ultra-
pasteurized)

1 cup dairy sour cream

Stir the cream and sour cream together thoroughly in a large bowl. Cover loosely with plastic wrap and let stand at room temperature overnight or until thickened, then refrigerate at least 4 hours more. (Keeps up to two weeks in the refrigerator.)

Víctoríano Huerta

> **"A host is like a general: it takes a mishap
> to reveal his genius."**
> **—HORACE**

VICTORIANO HUERTA (1854–1916), renowned Mexican general and dictator, was born of an Indian mother and *mestizo* father in Colotlan, Jalisco, northwest of Mexico City. At fifteen he started his military career when a general leading a convoy through Huerta's village took him on as his personal secretary, and later enrolled him in the Military College in Mexico City.

Distinguishing himself both in the office and in the field, Huerta rose gradually through the ranks, becoming a general in 1902. Nine years later Huerta took command of the troops fighting Emiliano Zapata and other revolutionaries. Tough and absolutely heartless, he was soon recognized as an able commander who was brutal in combat.

He was such an effective general that he succeeded in overthrowing President Francisco Madero's government in February 1913, and before you could say *arroz con pollo*, he appointed himself provisional president. He dissolved the congress and suppressed his opposition violently. Huerta's harsh and corrupt rule provoked continued revolutionary fighting in Mexico, which antagonized the U.S. administration of Woodrow Wilson. In April 1914, U.S. Marines landed at Veracruz and forced Huerta to resign a few months later. He eventually ended up in the U.S. Southwest and was arrested and charged with conspiring to violate the neutrality of the U.S. Released because of declining health, he died shortly thereafter in El Paso, Texas.

Huerta, always in search of a *fiesta*, entertained his military staff with long drinking bouts, and even as president he was more likely to be found performing his executive duties in the bars and cafés of Mexico City than in the National Palace.

T   H   E   •   R   E   C   I   P   E   S

Revolutionary Red Chile Salsa
Black Bean and Avocado Quesadillas
Turkey Breast with Mole Poblano
Banana and Pineapple Pudding

REVOLUTIONARY RED CHILE SALSA

4 *dried ancho chilies or*
   pasilla chilies
4 *medium tomatoes*
1 *medium onion, chopped*

1 *clove garlic, minced*
1 *teaspoon salt*
½ *teaspoon sugar*
1 *tablespoon cooking oil*

Cut chilies open, and discard stems and seeds. Cut chilies into small pieces, place in bowl, and cover with boiling water. Let stand 45 to 60 minutes. Drain.

To peel tomatoes, dip them in boiling water for 30 seconds, then plunge into cold water. Slip skins off. Quarter tomatoes. Place in blender, and blend till nearly smooth. Add the drained chilies. Add chopped onion, minced garlic, salt, and sugar; cover and blend till smooth.

In 1½ quart saucepan, combine tomato mixture and cooking oil. Cook and stir over medium heat about 10 minutes or till salsa is slightly thickened. Chill. Serve with corn tortilla chips. MAKES 2 CUPS

BLACK BEAN AND AVOCADO
QUESADILLAS

6 *flour tortillas*
refried black beans (see below)
1 *cup grated cheddar or Monterey Jack cheese*

1 *avocado, peeled, pitted, and sliced*
sour cream to garnish

Spread 3 of the tortillas with refried beans and top with grated cheese and avocado slices. Put 1 of the filled tortillas, filling side up, into a very hot, lightly oiled skillet. Top with a plain tortilla and cook for 1 minute, then flip the quesadilla over and cook 1 more minute. Repeat for the other 2 quesadillas. Cut each quesadilla pie-fashion into 6 slices. Serve with sour cream. SERVES 6.

REFRIED BLACK BEANS

2 *tablespoons olive or vegetable oil*
1 *small onion, finely chopped*
½ *green bell pepper, seeded and finely chopped*
1 *clove garlic, finely chopped*

1 *16-ounce can black beans, drained and pureed in blender or food processor*
½ *teaspoon dried oregano*
1 *teaspoon fresh cilantro, finely chopped*
pinch cayenne pepper

Sauté the onion and bell pepper in the olive oil over medium heat until they begin to brown, 4 or 5 minutes. Add the garlic and sauté for another minute. Add the pureéd black beans, oregano, and cilantro, and cook over medium heat, stirring constantly until the beans make a paste, about 5 minutes. Season with the cayenne pepper, stirring thoroughly. For the quesadillas, use hot or cooled to room temperature.

TURKEY BREAST
WITH MOLE POBLANO

6-pound turkey breast
1½ teaspoons salt
water
2 tablespoons cooking oil
2 medium tomatoes, chopped
1 medium onion, chopped
1 green chili pepper chopped
(optional)
½ cup blanched almonds
⅓ cup raisins
1 6-inch tortilla

2 tablespoons toasted sesame seeds
1 clove garlic
½ teaspoon dried, crushed red pepper
¼ teaspoon ground aniseed
¼ teaspoon ground cloves
½ teaspoon ground cinnamon
¼ teaspoon ground cilantro
dash of pepper
2 squares (1 ounce) melted
unsweetened chocolate
toasted sesame seeds to garnish

In Dutch oven, combine turkey breast, 1 teaspoon salt, and enough water to cover. Bring to boiling, then simmer 1½ hours or till meat is tender. Drain, reserving 1½ cups broth. Cool turkey slightly, then pat dry with paper toweling. In Dutch oven, brown the turkey breast in hot oil. Drain off fat.

To prepare *mole poblano*, combine reserved broth, chopped tomatoes, onion, chili pepper, almonds, raisins, cut-up tortilla, 2 tablespoons sesame seeds, garlic, red pepper, ½ teaspoon salt, aniseed, cloves, cinnamon, cilantro, and pepper in blender container. Cover and blend till nearly smooth. Stir in melted chocolate. Pour sauce over turkey breast in Dutch oven. Cover and simmer for 20 minutes or till heated through.

To serve, slice turkey breast; arrange on platter, spooning sauce on top. Sprinkle with toasted sesame seeds. SERVES 6-8.

BANANA AND PINEAPPLE PUDDING

2 *whole eggs*	4 *tablespoons rum*
2 *egg whites*	6 *thin slices of pound cake*
2 *cups milk*	1 *large banana, sliced*
½ *cup sugar*	1 *8¼ oz can pineapple chunks*

To make custard: beat 2 whole eggs in 1½ quart saucepan. Stir in milk and ¼ cup of sugar. Cook and stir over medium-low heat about 10 minutes or till mixture is slightly thickened and coats a metal spoon. Remove from heat, and stir in rum. Chill.

Line bottom and sides of a well-buttered 1½ quart dish with ladyfingered pound cake, cutting pieces as needed to fit. Arrange sliced banana and drained pineapple chunks over cake. Pour chilled custard over fruit.

To make meringue: beat 2 egg whites to soft peaks. Gradually add the remaining ¼ cup of sugar, beating to stiff peaks. Cover pudding with meringue. Bake 12 to 15 minutes at 325° or till meringue is golden. Serve chilled. SERVES 6

Jack the Ripper

" 'The man is a common murderer.' A common murderer,
possibly, but a very uncommon cook."
—SAKI

ACK THE RIPPER (late nineteenth century) is England's most notorious killer. From August to November 1888, Jack the Ripper operated within a square mile area in the East End slums of London, savagely murdering six to fourteen prostitutes.

The first known victim was murdered in Whitechapel on August 7, and the last known victim was murdered on November 10 in Spitalfields. The murders spread panic throughout London. Vigilante patrols were set up. Mass meetings were held attacking the Parliament, the home secretary, and the police commissioner for their laxity. After November 10, as mysteriously as they started, the murders suddenly stopped.

The Ripper was rumored to be a trained professional—a surgeon, a midwife, a butcher, or a barber—because of his skill with a knife. He was also rumored to be Queen Victoria's grandson, Prince Albert, or Eddy, as he was known. Despite the best efforts of Scotland Yard and endless speculation by both amateur and professional sleuths, his identity has never been discovered.

If the Ripper dined in the areas he roamed in, he would have certainly eaten pub food, some of the best food in London then and now. Even today tourists can go on walking tours in Whitechapel and the East End and see the exact spots where Jack the Ripper earned his name.

T H E · R E C I P E S

Lentil Soup
East End Fish and Chips
Savory Steak and Kidney Pie
Cleveland Street Bubble and Squeak
Trifle

LENTIL SOUP

2 *large onions, sliced*
1 *celery stalk, sliced*
1 *medium potato, sliced*
3 *slices bacon, diced*
1 *tablespoon butter*
1 *cup lentils*
1 *carrot*

4 *pork sausages (bangers), thickly sliced*
3 *teaspoons salt*
3 *quarts water*
1 *mutton chop (or lamb shank), cooked*
   malt vinegar

Place sliced onions, celery, potato, diced bacon, and butter in large, heavy pot. Cook until soft but not browned. Wash lentils, drain, and add to pot (presoaking is not necessary). Add sliced carrot, thickly sliced pork sausage, salt, and water. Add cooked mutton or lamb. Bring the water to a boil, lower heat, and simmer while covered for 3 hours or until lentils are soft. Add more water as needed; lentils absorb much of the water.

Pass the vinegar at table; a few dashes added to each serving will enhance flavor.
SERVES 6

EAST END FISH AND CHIPS

3 **pounds fresh fish fillets**
   (catch of the day)
3 **pounds baking potatoes, peeled**
   cooking oil
1½ **cup all-purpose flour**

2 **teaspoons salt**
6 **tablespoons water**
4 **egg yolks**
4 **stiffly beaten egg whites**
   malt vinegar

Cut fish into serving-size pieces. Pat dry with paper toweling.

Cut potatoes in uniform strips slightly larger than French fries. Fry in cooking oil at 375° till golden, about 5 to 6 minutes. Remove, drain, and keep warm.

To make batter, in a bowl, stir together 1¼ cups flour and 2 teaspoons salt. Make a well in center of dry ingredients. Add water, 3 tablespoons cooking oil, and egg yolks; beat smooth. Fold in egg whites. Dip fish in ¼ cup flour and then in batter. Fry fish in cooking oil at 375° till golden brown, about 1½ to 2 minutes on each side.

To serve, season fish and chips with salt and drizzle with malt vinegar. For authenticity, serve in cones made of rolled-up newspaper lined with wax paper. SERVES 6

SAVORY STEAK AND KIDNEY PIE

1 pound veal kidneys
2 pounds rump (or round) steak
1 cup claret wine (or other dry red wine)
2 onions
4 bay leaves
½ cup parsley
½ cup celery, diced
1 cup mushrooms, sliced

2 hard-boiled eggs
suet (or bacon drippings)
flour, for dredging and thickening
1 pint hot water
salt
1 teaspoon black pepper
1 teaspoon marjoram
1 pie crust dough, to cover casserole (see Blackbeard)

Separate the kidneys with a sharp knife, discarding all gristly portions and fat. Sprinkle with salt. Cover with claret, add bay leaves, 1 slice onion, and pepper. Let marinate for 2 hours.

Pound the steak with flour, then cut into 1-inch pieces. Brown suet in large skillet. Add diced onion and cook until clear; remove onion from skillet.

Over medium heat, brown steak well. Drain the kidneys, reserving the marinade; dredge with flour and brown, stirring carefully. Add 1 pint of hot water, stir well, then add chopped celery and parsley and marjoram.

Mix all ingredients well, and transfer to the casserole from which you intend to serve the pie. Strain in the marinade. Cover with a tight lid, and bake at 325° for about 1 hour.

Remove from oven. Brown the mushrooms in suet, and if thickening is needed, thicken with flour mixed in cold water and stirred carefully to avoid lumps. Add the mushrooms. Place 4 hard-boiled egg halves on top of mixture. Cover with pie crust (see Blackbeard), and return to oven. Bake at 400° until brown, about 20 to 30 minutes. Serve at once. SERVES 6

CLEVELAND STREET BUBBLE AND SQUEAK

3 cups mashed potatoes
2 cups Brussels sprouts
1 cup onions, chopped
2 cups frozen carrots and peas
½ lb bacon

1 teaspoon salt
½ teaspoon black pepper
3 dashes Worcestershire sauce
cooking oil

Prepare mashed potatoes, or leftovers are great if you have them. Cook Brussels sprouts in boiling water until crisp-tender. Cut in half. Add frozen carrots and peas and chopped onions and cook for 10 minutes, then drain all water. Add vegetables to premade mashed potatoes.

Fry bacon, allow to cool, and chop into small pieces. Add bacon, salt, pepper, and Worcestershire sauce to vegetables. Mix together slowly.

Heat cooking oil in heavy skillet. Roll potato mixture into patties, and cook until they "bubble and squeak." Serve warm. SERVES 6

TRIFLE

sponge cake (or jelly roll)
½ cup sherry (or brandy)
1 pint whipping cream
1 tablespoon sugar

custard (see below)
candied fruit (or shaved
   chocolate) for decoration

Line the bottom and sides of a deep dish with slices of sponge cake or jelly roll. Wet them with ⅓ cup sherry, and fill the dish nearly to the top with rich boiled custard.

Season ½ pint of heavy cream with 1 tablespoon sherry and 1 tablespoon sugar; whip to a froth, and lay it on the custard. Cover and decorate with the remaining ½ pint whipped cream, preserves of any kind, candied fruit or shaved chocolate. SERVES 6

CUSTARD

1 quart milk
½ cup cold milk
½ cup sugar

pinch of salt
6 eggs, whole
½ teaspoon vanilla extract

Scald 1 quart milk, then add ½ cup sugar and a pinch of salt. Beat 6 whole eggs, and add cold milk to them. Stir and gradually add to the hot milk mixture. Cook in top of double boiler until custard coats the spoon. When cold, add the vanilla flavoring.

General Custer

"Wish I had time for just one more bowl of chili."
—KIT CARSON

GEORGE ARMSTRONG CUSTER (1839–1876) was an American cavalry leader in both the Civil War and the campaigns of the western frontier. Born in New Rumley, Ohio, Custer graduated from West Point in 1861 — ranked thirty-fourth in a class of thirty-four. Because of the military opportunities of the Civil War, however, he became the youngest brigadier general in the Union Army, jumping rank, at the age of 23, over assorted captains, majors, and colonels, and proving that grades aren't everything.

Custer was noted for his bravery and daring during the Civil War, but it is for the Indian Wars in the West that Custer is best remembered. Always a headstrong young man, he was court-martialed in 1868 for disobeying orders and was suspended from the army for one year. After returning to duty from this enforced sabbatical, Custer quickly won a resounding victory over the Southern Cheyenne by destroying Chief Black Kettle and his entire village on the Washita River.

Black Kettle had wished for peaceful dealings with the white men and, as requested, had led his people into Indian Territory — now a part of the state of Oklahoma. On the morning of November 27, 1868, Custer's Seventh Cavalry bugler sounded the call to attack and Custer's men swooped down on Black Kettle's village, catching it off guard and achieving a swift and bloody victory.

On June 25, 1876, the odds changed. As Custer moved his troops down the slopes leading to the bank of the Little Bighorn River, Sitting Bull and Crazy Horse, leading their men, attacked the Seventh Cavalry from the rear. Custer

was so quickly surrounded that many of his soldiers did not have time to dismount or fight. Wave after wave of Sioux, some with guns, most with bows and arrows and clubs, swept over the besieged men. No white men survived the battle. The details of it, as well as Custer's conduct and character, will continue to stir controversy.

T H E • R E C I P E S
─────────

Trail Beans
Ham with Red-Eye Gravy
Short Ribs with Cornmeal Dumplings
Fried Soda Biscuits

TRAIL BEANS

2 cups dry pinto beans
7 cups cold water
2 pounds smoked ham hocks
1 large onion, chopped

1 6-ounce can tomato paste
1 4-ounce can green chili peppers
2 tablespoons sugar

Rinse pinto beans thoroughly. Combine beans and cold water in kettle and bring to boil. Simmer 2 minutes, remove from heat. Cover and let stand 1 hour. Do not drain.

Add ham hocks and onion. Cover and cook over low heat for 1 hour, stirring occasionally. Remove ham hocks. Remove meat from bones and discard bones. Return meat to beans. Add tomato paste, chopped chili peppers, and sugar. Cover and cook till beans are tender, about 30 minutes, stirring occasionally. SERVES 6

HAM WITH RED-EYE GRAVY

3 ½-inch thick country
    ham slices
⅔ cup water

1 teaspoon instant
    coffee powder

Trim the fat from ham and slice each ham in half. Cook trimmings in skillet until crisp. Discard trimmings, then brown ham in fat on both sides, 5 minutes per side.

Remove ham to warm platter. Stir water and instant coffee powder into drippings. Cook, scraping pan to remove crusty bits, for 2 to 3 minutes. Serve warm gravy over ham slices. SERVES 6

SHORT RIBS
WITH CORNMEAL DUMPLINGS

3 pounds beef short ribs
margarine
salt
pepper
1 medium onion, cut into thin wedges
1 clove garlic, minced
1 28-ounce can tomatoes, cut up
1 12-ounce can beer

1 fresh or dried hot red
   chili pepper, seeded
   and chopped
2 tablespoons vinegar
1 tablespoon sugar
¾ teaspoon salt
½ teaspoon ground nutmeg
   cornmeal dumplings (see below)

Trim fat from ribs and cut into serving-size pieces. Brown ribs on all sides, in heavy large skillet; season with salt and pepper. Drain off fat, reserving about 2 tablespoons. Add onion and garlic to drippings, and cook until onion is tender. Add tomatoes, beer, chili pepper, vinegar, sugar, and nutmeg. Return meat to skillet and bring to a boil. Reduce heat, simmer, covered, till meat is tender, about 2 hours. Cool and skim off excess fat. Return to heat; bring to boiling.

Drop dumpling batter by rounded tablespoonfuls into boiling stew mixture. Cover; simmer till dumplings are done, 10 to 12 minutes. SERVES 6

CORNMEAL DUMPLINGS

1 cup water
½ cup yellow cornmeal
½ teaspoon salt
1 egg, beaten

½ cup all-purpose flour
1 teaspoon baking powder
   dash of pepper
1 7-ounce can white corn

Combine water, cornmeal, and salt in saucepan. Bring to a boil. Cook and stir until thick. Remove from heat.

Stir small amount of hot mixture into 1 beaten egg, then return to hot mixture. In separate bowl stir together flour, baking powder, and pepper. Add to cornmeal and beat well. Stir in drained can of corn.

Add, as directed, to short ribs. SERVES 6

FRIED SODA BISCUITS

2 *cups all-purpose flour*	¼ *cup shortening*
1 *teaspoon baking soda*	¾ *cup buttermilk*
½ *teaspoon salt*	*shortening*

Stir together flour, soda, and salt. Cut in shortening until the mixture resembles coarse crumbs. Make a well in the dry mixture and add buttermilk all at once. Stir until the dough clings together. Knead gently on lightly floured surface.

Melt enough shortening in deep skillet to give a depth of 1 inch and heat to 375°. To shape each biscuit, cut off about 1 tablespoon of the dough, and form piece into a ball about 1 inch in diameter. Flatten slightly. Place biscuits a few at a time in the hot shortening. Fry till golden, turning once, about 2 minutes per side. Drain on paper toweling. Serve hot. SERVES 6

Rasputín

"Someone said of a very great egoist: 'He would burn your house down to cook himself a couple of eggs.' "
—NICHOLAS CHAMFORT

ASPUTIN (1872–1916), also known as the "Mad Monk," was a Russian mystic who gained influence over the tsarina Alexandra Fyodorovna after supposedly curing her only son, Alexis, of hemophilia. Originally surnamed Novykh, he was born to a peasant family in Siberia. As he spent much of his youth in drink and debauchery, he came to be called Rasputin, which means "debaucher."

Despite his womanizing and drinking, he entered the church and gained a widespread reputation as a faith healer. In 1907 he made his way into the Imperial Court, where he quickly became a favorite of the tsarina and, through her, influenced Nicholas II, the tsar. Rasputin's control over the imperial family further eroded its prestige and was instrumental in bringing about the collapse of the Romanov dynasty.

When the tsar took direct command of the Russian troops in 1915, Alexandra and Rasputin were in complete control of the government. Several conservative noblemen, disturbed by Rasputin's destructive influence on the already deteriorating government, assassinated him. First they poisoned him, then they shot him, and then they stabbed him. When this failed to slow him down, the thoroughly frustrated assassins tied chains to his body and drowned him in the Neva River. The last tactic worked. We think.

But before his unfortunate end, life was good for Rasputin. Lunch at the palace with Nicholas and Alexandra was an elegant and elaborate affair, with up to twenty people at the table and four or five courses. Like the tsar, Rasputin never touched caviar, since he had upset his stomach once by eating too much of it. The "Mad Monk" preferred simple Russian dishes (the only tie he kept to his childhood in Siberia), such as cabbage and sauerkraut soups, and he was very partial to suckling pig.

THE • RECIPES
──────────

Peasant Salad
Sauerkraut Soup
Imperial Court Beef Stroganoff
Noodles Romanov
Mystic's Eggplant Caviar
Alexandra's Favorite Sweetie

PEASANT SALAD

2 *large beets*
2 *large potatoes*
8 *ounces dried salt cod*
4 *ounces shallots*
2 *cloves garlic*
2 *medium-sized tomatoes*
1 *tablespoon chopped parsley*

¼ *teaspoon white pepper*
3 *tablespoons vinegar*
⅔ *cup olive oil*
6 *tablespoons water*
4 *hard-cooked eggs*
¾ *cup ripe olives*

Rinse the beets and potatoes under cold running water. Cook the beets in boiling water for about 1 hour, or until tender. Drain and peel. Cook the potatoes in boiling water for about 25 minutes. Drain and peel. Slice the beets and potatoes into rounds about ½-inch thick, and place in a deep salad bowl.

Place the cod in a roasting pan, and bake in a preheated 400° oven for 15 minutes. When the cod is cool, remove the bones. Flake the fish, and place in a bowl under cold running water to remove the salt.

Peel and chop shallots, garlic, and tomatoes, then mix with parsley, pepper, vinegar, oil, and water; and beat well.

Drain the cod thoroughly, then place in the bowl with the beets and potatoes and sprinkle with the tomato mixture. Toss lightly. Garnish the salad with slices of egg and the ripe olives. Serve chilled. SERVES 6

SAUERKRAUT SOUP

1½ **pounds sauerkraut**	2 **tablespoons flour**
6 **slices bacon**	½ **pound smoked sausages**
2 **cups onions**	¼ **cup sour cream**

If canned sauerkraut is used, drain it and reserve the juice. Put sauerkraut in a colander and rinse under cold running water for a few minutes. Measure the juice, and add enough water to make 6 cups. Combine liquid with the sauerkraut in a large saucepan. Bring to a boil, and cook over low heat.

Brown bacon in a skillet, then remove and reserve. Pour off all but ¼ cup of the fat, and sauté the onions until brown. Blend in the flour until browned. Mix in a little of the soup, then add this mixture to all the soup. Slice the sausages, and brown them. Drain, and add the sausages to soup. Cook over low heat for 45 minutes. Taste for seasoning. Crumble the bacon into the soup, then stir in the sour cream. SERVES 6

IMPERIAL COURT BEEF STROGANOFF

2 *pounds beef sirloin steak*	1 *clove garlic, minced*
4 *tablespoons all-purpose flour*	2 *tablespoons tomato paste*
½ *teaspoon salt*	1 *10½-ounce can condensed*
4 *tablespoons margarine*	*beef broth (or bouillon)*
2 *3-ounce cans sliced mushrooms,*	1½ *cups dairy sour cream*
drained	4 *tablespoons dry white wine*
¾ *cup onion, chopped*	

Cut beef into thin strips, then coat with mixture of 1 tablespoon flour and salt. In a skillet, brown beef strips quickly in 2 tablespoons margarine. Add drained mushrooms, chopped onion, and minced garlic; cook till onion is crisp-tender, or about 3 minutes. Remove meat and mushrooms from pan. Add 2 tablespoons margarine to pan drippings, then blend in 3 tablespoons flour. Add tomato paste. Stir in broth.

Cook and stir over medium heat till thickened and bubbly. Return meat and mushrooms to skillet. Stir in sour cream and dry white wine, then cook slowly till heated through (*do not boil*). Serve with Noodles Romanov. SERVES 6

Note: Russian sour cream is thinner than the usual commercial packaged varieties. The thicker versions have a high fat content and separate quickly when cooked. Blend three parts commercial sour cream to one part half-and-half, or use half-and-half sour cream as a substitute. (Never use nondairy or other adulterated forms of sour cream, only the real thing).

NOODLES ROMANOV

¾ *cup onion, chopped*
3 *tablespoons butter*
3 *tablespoons flour*
1½ *teaspoons salt*
½ *teaspoon Dijon mustard*
1½ *cups cottage cheese*
¾ *cup grated cheddar cheese*

3 *teaspoons lemon juice*
pepper
1 *cup powdered milk*
1½ *cup water*
1 *pound dry egg noodles*
¼ *cup chopped parsley*

Sauté chopped onion in butter until tender. Stir in flour, salt, and pepper until smooth. Combine powdered milk with water, then add to sauce with mustard.

Cook, stirring, until thickened. Stir in cheeses and lemon juice, then cooked noodles. Pour into greased casserole dish and bake, uncovered, at 350° for 40 to 45 minutes. Sprinkle with parsley, and serve hot. SERVES 6

MYSTIC'S EGGPLANT CAVIAR

1 *large eggplant (2 pounds)*
1 *cup onion, finely chopped*
¾ *cup green pepper, finely chopped*
3 *tablespoons cooking oil*

1 *6-ounce can tomato paste*
1½ *teaspoons salt*
½ *teaspoon pepper*
assorted crackers

Cook whole eggplant in boiling water till tender, about 25 minutes. Cool, peel, and finely chop. In medium skillet, cook finely chopped onion and green pepper in oil till tender but not brown. Add tomato paste, salt, and pepper. Simmer for 5 minutes. Added chopped eggplant, then simmer uncovered for 30 minutes, stirring often. (Add more oil if eggplant sticks.) Chill. Serve with crackers. SERVES 6

ALEXANDRA'S FAVORITE SWEETIE

2 *cups dry cottage cheese*
½ *cup sugar*
½ *cup unsalted butter*
1 *egg yolk*

½ *cup dairy sour cream*
¼ *cup almonds, finely chopped*
½ *teaspoon vanilla*
½ *cup white raisins*

Push cottage cheese through a sieve. Combine sugar, butter, and egg yolk in bowl, then blend in cottage cheese. Stir in sour cream, finely chopped nuts, and vanilla. Press mixture into 4-cup mold. Cover and chill overnight. Unmold and garnish with raisins.
SERVES 6

Al Capone

"Leave the gun. Take the cannolis."
—**Clemenza**, *in the movie,* **The Godfather**

I T WAS SAID in the 20s that if you couldn't get a job in Chicago, you couldn't get a job anywhere. Al Capone (1899–1947) found work almost immediately when he arrived there at the age of twenty-one. After a little time and a few rival gang shootings, Capone, an extremely industrious and innovative bad guy, controlled most of the criminal activities in town.

Capone's gunmen were credited with the St. Valentine's Day Massacre in 1929, when six members of the Bugs Moran gang and an "innocent" bystander were murdered in a Northside garage. The charges were never successfully pinned on Al Capone, but two years later he was convicted of income-tax evasion and served eight years in prison.

The worst meal Capone ate out of choice was as a guest of the mayor of Philadelphia while on the run from a Chicago gang with revenge on its agenda. After a night under lock and key for his own protection, he dined on bologna, dry bread, and coffee in the morning, safe but hardly satisfied.

Capone's own gastronomic specialty was created in his family home, apron around his neck, a $50,000, eleven-and-a-half carat diamond ring sparkling. His authentic Italian spaghetti was always served with Chianti, although Capone himself perhaps preferred a scotch-and-water. His mother, Theresa Capone, was the main chef, however, and conveniently lived in the second flat of his two-flat brick house on Chicago's South Side. The recipes included here are hers; hearty, delicious Italian fare, no doubt instrumental in giving Al Capone the energy and enthusiasm he needed to run Chicago.

T H E • R E C I P E S

Fresh Vegetable Salad
Mom's Baked Lasagna
Al's Spaghetti Sauce
South Side Sautéed Chicken
St. Valentine's Day Sugar Cookies
Parmesan Garlic Bread
Raspberry Italian Ice

FRESH VEGETABLE SALAD

½ pound fresh asparagus
   Italian salad dressing (see below)
½ pound fresh chickpeas
4 hard-boiled eggs, chopped
½ cup pimiento-stuffed
   green olives

½ cup ripe black olives
   (pitted)
2 cucumbers, sliced
½ pound fresh mushrooms, sliced
1 cup salad tomatoes, sliced
1 head of lettuce

Wash the asparagus and break off stalks. Remove scales with a knife, then wash again. Place in a saucepan and add 1 inch boiling, salted water. Bring to boiling and cook for 5 minutes. Reduce heat and cover. Cook for 15 minutes or until asparagus is crisp-tender, then drain. Cover with Italian salad dressing and chill overnight.

Cook the chickpeas in boiling, salted water until crisp-tender, then drain. Chill. Drain the asparagus, and reserve salad dressing. Arrange the asparagus, chopped eggs, green olives, ripe olives, sliced cucumbers, mushrooms, tomatoes, and chickpeas on a lettuce-lined platter. Serve cold with reserved dressing.

ITALIAN SALAD DRESSING

3 ounces white wine vinegar
   salt
   black pepper

7 ounces olive oil
4 garlic cloves, pressed
1½ tablespoons tarragon

Mix vinegar with pressed garlic and tarragon, and salt and pepper to taste. Add oil, and beat with fork. Let stand for 30 minutes to blend flavors.

MOM'S BAKED LASAGNA

½ pound Italian sausage
½ pound ground beef
1 clove garlic, minced
½ teaspoon salt
½ cup dry red wine
2 pints spaghetti sauce
1 6-ounce can tomato paste

1 16-ounce package lasagna
2 eggs, slightly beaten
2 cups ricotta cheese
½ cup grated Parmesan cheese
2 tablespoons parsley flakes
dash of black pepper
1 pound mozzarella cheese,
thinly sliced

Brown meat in large skillet, then drain off excess fat. Add minced garlic, salt, and wine. Simmer for 5 minutes, then stir in spaghetti sauce and tomato paste; cook, stirring occasionally, for 10 to 15 minutes.

For lasagna noodles, boil four quarts water. Drop noodles one at a time into boiling water. Cook for 5 minutes, stirring with wooden spoon. Drain and rinse with cold water.

In bowl, combine slightly beaten eggs, ricotta cheese, Parmesan cheese, parsley, and pepper. Blend well. In a greased 13-inch x 9-inch pan, arrange a layer of lasagna, spread with ricotta mixture, then add a layer of meat sauce, and a layer of sliced mozzarella. Repeat until all ingredients are used. (Use a layer of sauce only on top.)

Bake at 350° for 30 minutes or until bubbly. Let stand 10 minutes before serving.
SERVES 6 PLUS*

*Al's mother, Mrs. Capone, always made enough lasagna so that "Little Al" would have some left over to take home with him.

AL'S SPAGHETTI SAUCE

2 pounds ground beef
1 small onion, finely chopped
    olive oil
½ green pepper, finely chopped
1 15-ounce can tomato sauce
2 12-ounce cans tomato paste
1 cup fresh mushrooms, chopped
1 cup water

½ cup red wine
2 teaspoons salt
1 teaspoon black pepper
1 teaspoon oregano
1 teaspoon thyme
½ teaspoon basil
2 garlic cloves
1 bay leaf

Combine meat and finely chopped onion in pan. Cook until meat is brown and onion is tender. Drain excess fat.

Add finely chopped green pepper and all other ingredients. Cover and simmer for 1½ hours. Uncover and simmer an additional ½ hour or until sauce is thick. Occasionally stir during cooking. MAKES 1½ QUARTS

Note: For the spaghetti sauce, Theresa Capone preferred fresh tomatoes (3½ to 4 pounds at 25 cents a pound at Stop & Shop, a block west of State Street on Washington, telephone RAndolph 8500: "Come to the store or phone your order. We have regular deliveries to most parts of Chicago."

Al, with a busy schedule and a man of action, preferred canned tomatoes (three no. 2 size cans for 25 cents, at Hillmans, 30 West Washington Street, no deliveries. ("Slippery" Frank Rio would pick them up on his way back from leaving bribes at nearby City Hall.)

SOUTHSIDE SAUTÉED CHICKEN

¾ *pound small white onions*
   3½-pound chicken
¼ *cup olive oil*
2 *tablespoons butter*
1½ *teaspoons salt*
½ *teaspoon black pepper*
1 *clove garlic, minced*

1 *cup dry white wine*
1½ *cups tomatoes, peeled and diced*
3 *tablespoons parsley, chopped*
½ *teaspoon basil*
½ *cup chicken broth*
   (or bouillon)
½ *pound sweet Italian sausages*

Cook the peeled onions in boiling water for 5 minutes, then drain and dry. Wash and dry the chicken. Heat the oil and butter in a skillet, then brown the disjointed chicken and onions. Add the salt, pepper, minced garlic, and wine, then cook over medium heat until almost all the wine is evaporated. Mix in the peeled and diced tomatoes, chopped parsley, basil, and broth. Cover and cook over low heat for 30 minutes.

While the chicken is cooking, cut the sausages into 1-inch slices. Brown them in a skillet, drain, and add to the chicken after it has cooked for 30 minutes. Cook 10 minutes longer or until the chicken is tender. Serve hot. SERVES 6

ST. VALENTINE'S DAY
SUGAR COOKIES

2 *cups flour (approximately)*	1 *cup sugar*
1½ *teaspoons baking powder*	1 *egg*
½ *teaspoon salt*	1 *teaspoon vanilla extract*
½ *cup butter*	1 *tablespoon cream (or milk)*

Preheat oven to 375°. Sift 1½ cups flour with baking powder and salt.

Cream butter until soft, then beat in sugar, egg, vanilla, and cream. Stir in flour mixture. Add enough remaining flour to make dough stiff enough to roll out. Refrigerate until well chilled.

Place dough on lightly floured board; roll about ⅛-inch thick. Cut into heart shapes with floured cutter or knife. Place on ungreased baking sheets and sprinkle with sugar. Bake 8 to 10 minutes in preheated oven (375°). Remove to cooling trays. Can be served plain or decorated with red-food-colored sugar. MAKES 25

PARMESAN GARLIC BREAD

2 loaves Italian bread
1 cup butter
2 teaspoons parsley flakes
½ teaspoon crumbled oregano

½ teaspoon dried dillweed
2 garlic cloves, minced
grated Parmesan cheese

Cut bread diagonally into 1½ inch slices; do not cut all the way through.

Mix soft butter, 1 teaspoon parsley, oregano, dillweed, and minced garlic. Spread mixture on both sides of bread slices.

Shape aluminum foil around loaves, and twist ends, leaving tops open, Sprinkle tops liberally with Parmesan cheese and remaining parsley flakes. Heat in 400° oven for 10 minutes. Serve warm. SERVES 6

RASPBERRY ITALIAN ICE

3 cups ripe raspberries
2 lemons

3 cups water
4¼ cups sugar

Rub fruit through sieve, and add juice of lemons. Set aside.

Place water and sugar in large pot over low heat. Heat until sugar dissolves; raise temperature for slow, rolling boil. Reduce heat, and simmer for 3 minutes.

Let sugar syrup cool, then combine with raspberry mixture. Pour into plastic container and freeze. Serve very cold. SERVES 6

ACKNOWLEDGMENTS

In the course of writing *Cooking with the Bad Guys,* I had indispensable help from my wife, Frankie, whose contributions I gratefully acknowledge. Unstinting with her time researching, giving creative input, structuring and organizing, and we always had time to share a laugh.

Special thanks to my editor, Tracy Carns, editorial director of The Overlook Press who, undaunted, made the original manuscript work; thanks also to production manager Michael Hornburg, designer Bernard Schleifer and publicity manager Gene Taft for their contributions and expertise.

And special tribute to my fellow cooks and tasters: my sons Zachary and Don, Marge and Jack White, Gladys Lansing, Sigried Jensen Abel, Olga Kaehler, Dr. John Youngpeter, Limei and Ding Deng, Ling Ye, Sonia and Freddy Ganteaume, Hiroshi and Hiroko Saito, Starfish Angela and, rest his kind soul, "Porter" the railroad cook who knew the real gritty on George Armstrong Custer and Alphonse Capone.